To Geo

A flame [illegible] [illegible]

sleep,

xx Fran

Soul Journeys Series

A Fairy's TALE

Fran Laurie Olsen

Endorsements for Soul Journeys Series: A Fairy's Tale

A Fairy's Tale is at once playful and profound; a mixture of personal story, reflection, wisdom, philosophy, and deep spiritual insights. Fran's wisdom, interspersed with profound poetry from other mystics, leads us into deep places of reflection on life and its meaning, all in a playful, "lightening up" way. Fairy tales are sources of true wisdom, as Einstein knew. This one is no exception.

Rev. Sharon Moon, (United Church), author of *The Healing Oasis* and *Returning to the Oasis: Guided Meditations for Body, Mind and Spirit*

"Once upon a time there was a wise woman who wrote a beautiful story of her Higher Self, a flower fairy, who lives steadfastly within her, despite all of life's obstacles and cruel losses. Part memoir, part active imagination, Olsen's life story and musings upon it, provide a treasure trove of inspiration and it encourages us to reflect on our own experiences and expand our perspectives on the meaning of life."

Dr. Mary Harsany, (Psychologist) Co-President,
The C.G. Jung Society of Montreal

"Fran Olsen has evoked a world of poetry and fairies from her personal journey. This beautifully and optimistically rendered work/play comes straight from the heart and the spirit."

Murray Shugar, Editor, The C.G. Jung Society of Montreal.

"A Fairy's Tale by Fran Laurie Olsen is an enchanting story of two lives.

As a human child, the author remembers a deep yearning and longing for wholeness, for connection -- to feel a part of something bigger than herself.

The book starts by telling us: "Most of my life I have lived as a flower fairy, a daisy flower fairy to be precise." This conviction gave her the certain knowledge that "plants and animals are highly intelligent".

The story contains a fine balance between lightness and heaviness, both of which she has experienced. Lightness as a fairy, heaviness in a human world where she is all too familiar with hoarding emotions, with carrying layers of pain and hurts reaching back through generations.

It was the death, not only of her first husband but of several other friends and relatives that seemed to be the source of a flood of images and poems that came pouring out of her creative imagination. She learned to "trust the process" though it may look and feel like a shattering…

Her purpose has been to bring her fairy magic into human form for the enhancement and pleasure of All-That-Is.

Read this book. It will intrigue and fascinate you. The illustrations are well chosen and enhance the story. It will fill you with the intriguing possibilities of what you too could imagine and express. It challenges us to dare a little. Try it and see."

Clare Hallward, Editor of *David Steindl-Rast: Essentials Writings (2010)* and former Chair and Board Member of the Thomas More Institute, Montreal.

"This delightful book presents insights into our spiritual nature and the way that consciousness works through the physical world. It is a story told from the perspective of a daisy flower fairy that has chosen to incarnate as a human being, and relates her experiences of being a woman, as perceived from this fairy viewpoint. Having worked with deva and elemental beings for many years I know that such experiences are possible, so this for me was a very believable story, showing a depth and insight into the spiritual nature of the world we inhabit."

David Furlong has been a spiritual teacher and a therapist for more than forty-five years. He is the author of several books including *'Working With Earth Energies,'* which relates his experiences with the deva, elemental and nature kingdoms.

"A delightful, imaginative tale illustrating Fran Olsen's epic adventure of self-discovery. A story of her relentless search for inner wisdom and the not-yet-visible yielding fairy-like authenticity beyond layers of human alienation. A tale that beautifully portrays the archetypal journey to wholeness - the quest to find the integral unity of our true nature."

Stephen Sims, author of *River of Awareness* and *The Wisdom of Authenticity.*

FriesenPress

Suite 300 - 990 Fort St
Victoria, BC, Canada, V8V 3K2
www.friesenpress.com

First Edition — 2015

ISBN
978-1-4602-6704-2 (Paperback)
978-1-4602-6705-9 (eBook)

1. Self-Help, Personal Growth

Distributed to the trade by The Ingram Book Company

Cover Design by Ana Maria Cano.

Web site www.friesenpress.com

For our grandchildren, Anna and Markus Segelken

My first yoga teacher, Rose Rosenstone

And my little friends, William Choy-Monaco,
Sophia and Maya Phaneuf-Morrisette, Elsa Strong,
Sasha and Sophia Stoger-Von Bauer, and Maia Shrouder
may you grow up knowing you have wings!

"Your vision will become clear only when you
can look into your own heart.
Who looks outside, dreams; who looks inside, awakes."

"As a child I felt myself to be alone, and I am still, because I know things
and must hint at things which others apparently know nothing of,
and for the most part do not want to know.
Loneliness does come from having no people about one,
but from being unable to communicate the things
that seem important to oneself..."

C.G. Jung, Memories, Dreams, Reflections

The Guest House

This being human is a guest house.
Every morning a new arrival.

A joy, a depression, a meanness,
some momentary awareness comes
as an unexpected visitor.

Welcome and entertain them all!
Even if they are a crowd of sorrows,
who violently sweep your house
empty of its furniture,
still, treat each guest honorably.
He may be clearing you out
for some new delight.

The dark thought, the shame, the malice.
meet them at the door laughing and invite them in.

Be grateful for whatever comes.
because each has been sent
as a guide from beyond.

Jelaluddin Rumi, Coleman Barks, translator

Table of Contents

* Words appearing with an asterisk are defined in the End Notes

Gratitudes

When I decided to publish this story, I was very fortunate to have reconnected with one of my closest friends from high school. Sheila Leigh and I had been put in touch through a high school reunion search, and while we live at opposite ends of the country, we have continued to be connected. She had become an editor and agreed to help me. She has gently and lovingly guided me in editing this book. We've managed to get together to spend some in-depth times on it during my husband's and my visits to our grandchildren out West. Sheila's wise and loving energy, together with her own deep understanding of what this book is about, has helped me immensely and she has been a mid-wife to its manifestation.

Another friend, to whom I am eternally grateful, is Ana Maria Cano, a graphic designer, who managed to squeeze out some time in her busy schedule to design this lovely book cover. I knew she would come up with just the right thing. Obrigado tão muito, o seu esforço extraordinário é tão apreciado.

My high school English teacher, John Howes, and his dear wife, Didi, have become close friends and he has spent many hours reading, re-reading, and making suggestions, thank you both for being there. Others who have read it and picked up typos, or made suggestions are Margaret

Goldik, Diane Tegtmeier, Markus Werner, Barbara Feldman, and Wendy Ball (Prem Nartan). Special thanks to Mary Swaine who let me use her atelier way back in 1995 and it was here I learned to go with the flow of creativity. Thank you as well to young Sybil Randy for literally lending me her hand for the picture "Trying to Reach Back to the Fairy Realms".

Without the inspiration and constant teachings from the Natural World, this book would perhaps not have happened. I have been such an unwilling collaborator at times, allowing fear and busyness to overpower the spirit that would speak through me. It is the spirit of "All-That-Is" that asks us to *wake up, to listen, and to see,* and I am humbled and grateful for its voice in me, and the words that come to me.

I am always indebted to the love, patience, and support that I receive daily from my husband, Rick Sheffer. He has heard, or read, this manuscript many times. He always "has my back". I'd also like to thank our children Alex and Chris Olsen and Megan and Stephen Sheffer, as well as my sister, Libby Monaco, for their support and encouragement.

I am grateful for the lives of those who are now deceased, for my parents' love; Mother's faith in action, her squashing and discipline, which taught me to be strong, and Father's gentleness and passion for flowers, which taught me to see Beauty and to connect with the Natural World and for my first husband, Bill Olsen, who taught me so much and who died too young.

They say it takes a village to raise a child; well it takes a community of dear friends to buoy one up and help to see these projects through to the end. I have been so encouraged by many dear friends, my "Soul Sisters", Claire Hallward, Kathy Camozzi, Réjane Mercier, Sandra Doig, Sharon Moon and Sophie Slade. Others that have provided a listening ear or words of support are: Ann Molnar,

Susan & Marc Phaneuf, Nina Stein, Graziella Malagoni., Prem Nartan (Wendy Ball), Helen Ryf, Bevan Skerratt, Hannelore Moebius, Margaret Zurbrigg, Surinder Kallar, Steve Sims, Roland Berard, Tobie Steinhouse, Betty Jaques, Gita Beattie, Allyna Harris, Lynn & Dick Hovey, Heide Shrouder, Annemarie Shrouder, Elin Gustafson, Harriet Gustafson, Joanne Ransom, Crystal Hooper, Jeanne Taylor and Carmen Blake. I'd also like to thank those who have taken the time to read the book and write an endorsement for me, it has been very encouraging for me as I've moved along in the publishing process. In particular, I'd like to thank Judith Duerk for kindly agreeing to write the foreword to this book. Her kind and insightful words have affected me deeply. I have long been an admirer of her writings and have used them in woman's groups and retreats over the years. She is truly a kindred spirit.

I am also indebted to those poets and their translators, for the wonderful excerpts I have been given permission to use, they have added so much to my book.

I have had some truly wonderful and inspiring teachers, including my first yoga teacher, Rose Rosenstone, as well as, Sister Meryl Pedersen (PRH), Dr. Tom Francoeur, Zen Master, Thich Nhat Hanh, and more recently, Barbara Marx Hubbard. I thank you all for your wisdom, love, and encouragement.

There have been others who have helped or encouraged me over the years, including a number of my clients and yoga students who shall remain unnamed, but you know who you are. I am so grateful for the richness you brought to my life and I thank all of you.

A special thank you to Jade, Kevin and Jean Marc at Photosynthèse, atelier d'art graphique for their patient assistance and suggestions in the reproduction of my illustrations.

A big thank you to the people I have worked with at Freisen Press, in particular Galia Zavgorodni, Daimon Moore and the editors and designers that have helped me to get this little book out there.

Most of all, I am grateful to *Great Mystery* for "All-That-Is".

Foreword

I found myself reaching out, wanting to connect with the daisy flower-fairy self of Fran Olsen and reconnect with my own flower-fairy self and realizing how closely connected the two selves of Fran Olsen were -- the flower-fairy and the human self. How easily she seemed able to slip back and forth between the two selves!

Oh, if only she had shared with her readers how she was able to do this, so that we also, might transition with such ease!

So much of modern life seems calculated to make us fit into what Ms. Olsen called "prison," the world of school and work, with little chance of understanding that all of a flower's petals do not need to be exactly the same and perfectly matched, and that all flowers can be seen as beautiful just as they are -- that it is their irregularities that help make them so appealing.

Oh, if only we here in the human realm could be taught this and helped to feel more secure about our own unevenness and irregularities! Do you suppose we would stop twisting ourselves into a tangle, stop trying to be what we are not, and end up with less unhappiness, strife, and war in the world?

This is only one of the many cosmic questions that Fran Olsen addresses in her book. If I read every page slowly and thoughtfully and really allow myself to take in what is presented here, I can see that there are suggestions of how to befriend and care for the earth Herself and even how to let Her know that we truly care for Her and honor Her.

So, may I recommend to you, Reader, to allow yourself to go slowly and thoughtfully through every single page, and to not dismiss anything as just fanciful or without serious and worthy substance.

In fact, how wonderful to have this gift from Fran Olsen that addresses so many weighty issues and problems with a bit of lightness and a lovely touch of fancy. May it bless you as you read, as it is blessing me each day as I read and re-read it...even...more...slowly.

Judith Duerk 22nd May, 2015

Preface

So here's the thing, I'm a sixty-something-year-old professional woman and I awaken one morning with a sentence in my head. I think to myself, *I must have been dreaming*, but the words stay there; they don't fade away. I do write poetry from time to time and often a poem lets me know it's there, by a word, or phrase, hanging around in my mind. When this happens I write it down and then the entire poem comes, like a baby, all in one piece—fully formed. So I say to myself, "better write this down". Here is the sentence exactly as I wrote it:

I have lived most of my life as a flower fairy, a daisy flower fairy to be precise.

No sooner had I written down these words than an entire story wrote itself, flowing freely from my pen. I have been sitting on this tale for almost seven years now, wondering what to do with it. From time to time my inner voice has instructed me to add little bits here and there, to amplify certain ideas, and I've done that.

The fairy takes on a human child's voice at the beginning (a wise-beyond-her-years voice, mind you) then grows into an adult voice as the years pass. Now the time has come to share her story with the world, so I give you............"A Fairy's Tale".

Chapter One

"Crossings"

All is empty, brilliant,
perfect in its own being.
In the world of things as they are,
there is no self, no non-self.
If you want to describe its essence,
the best you can say is "Not-two".
In this "Not-two" nothing is separate,
and nothing in the world is excluded.
The enlightened of all times and places
have entered into this truth.

Being is an aspect of non-being;
non-being is no different from being.
Until you understand this truth,
you won't see anything clearly.
One is all; all
are one. When you realize this,
what reason for holiness or wisdom?

Seng-Ts'an (?-606)

Most of my life I have lived as a flower fairy, a daisy flower fairy to be precise. My name in the fairy realms is hard to express, but roughly translated it means, "one who dances with the wind" and I was sometimes called *Winddancer.* I love that! I was also known as Filanthy, which means "friend of flowers". In the realm of *nature spirits,* fairies are considered to be *earth angels.* Just as celestial angels are in charge of watching over humans and helping them, *earth angels* (fairies), together with other elementals, are in charge of watching over the Natural World of plants and animals. In helping to create Beauty in *nature,* flower fairies are particularly focused on flowering plants. As *daisy flower fairies,* we are very connected to this group and reflect some of the qualities of daisies. We are a kind of a breed of our own, and a little wild, like gypsies really. We wander all over, planting ourselves wherever, and feeling free to move on and relocate at any time. No ties. You know what I mean? Although we mostly travel in small groups, sometimes we move on alone. We get along pretty easily with others when we move into a space. We tend to fit in and around them; we don't crowd them out, and we kind of enhance what they're doing. I'd say that as a species we're mostly well-liked and well-received. Others see us as fresh, dainty-yet-sturdy, and long-lasting. The species we are closest to in the Natural World would be butterflies, but we're also like humans in many ways.

I really loved this life with my people. We got to do some really interesting things and to see some amazing places. I liked being with my own kind, feeling part of a large family-like group while still mixing with others of all types. We were entirely part of and interdependent with Nature. Peace, Harmony, Creativity, Beauty, and Love were the guiding principals for all of us.

Because of our great freedom and natural friendliness, we tended to connect with human children. Many of them could easily see us, and we liked playing with them. Perhaps that's how it all came about. I got too close to a human: a little girl. We became the best of friends. We really loved each other. I began to wonder what it would be like to be a human. Wonderful as my life was, to me, being a human looked even more exciting. She, on the other hand, thought that being a flower fairy, particularly a daisy flower fairy, would be the most fantastic experience in the world, (or "out of the world"). So, out of love, we decided that we'd switch places on the next *turning of life.*

Today, I am living a human existence and want it written down, lest I forget the deep knowledge I still remember—memories I have from my previous life and the experiences I'm having now in human form. You might find this all hard to believe, because I seem young, but you must remember that I've had a very long life on the other side and so am much wiser than my years as a human.

While fairies are in touch with the so-called, "non-physical world", and are well versed in its ways, we are ever so slightly more solid, while still being airy and therefore can cross over the invisible line to become human. But we need to find a human who is willing to change places with us, and then we can easily slip into the denser world of humans, or vice versa into the *not-yet-visible world* of nature spirits. This is how I came to be born in the human realms. Sometimes I look at pictures of myself when I was really little and think I'm kind of funny looking. By age two I had to wear these round, wire glasses because one of my eyes had turned in and the other was weak. So this is the story of what it has been like to be a daisy flower fairy, now living a human existence.

The glasses

Chapter Two

"Transitions"

What will our children do in the morning?
Will they wake with their hearts wanting to play, the way wings should?
Will they have dreamed the needed flights and gath-
ered the strength from the planets
That all men and women need to balance the
wonderful charms of the earth
So that her power and beauty does not make us forget our own?
I know all the ways of the heart – how it wants to be alive.

Love so needs to love that it will endure almost anything,
even abuse, just to flicker for a moment.
But the sky's mouth is kind, its song will never
hurt you, for I sing those words.
What will our children do in the morning if they do not see us fly?

Rumi (1207-1273)

Humans react very strangely to any kind of "imperfection" in children. They see a child like me as "defective" and tend to look away quickly, or stare with a look of pity. What a silly way to be! The flowers often have various imperfections, one petal smaller or larger, some maybe not fully formed, or missing altogether. In fact, a flower with perfect petals, all uniform, is just about impossible to find! Another crazy thing that humans do is to consider some children more beautiful than others. They make a lot of comparisons and even consider some species ("races" they call them) more delightful to the eye than others. This is truly absurd! They don't seem to be able to see Beauty in each person.

All flowers are seen as beautiful just as they are. What's more, it is their irregularities that make them so appealing. Silk flowers, with each petal identical to the next, are less attractive, because perfection is not really about uniformity. It is about being perfectly you, with all those endearing variations that no one else quite captures.

Flower fairies only see Beauty. Beauty is the mother of "All-That-Is". She is in everyone and everything. Just as Love is the father of All-That-Is. Actually, when Love and Love's reflection, Beauty, joined, All-That-Is was born, or one might say **manifested.* The conditions were right for the great "unmanifest" to manifest and the flame of that union is burning, still.

I'm not so sure I like being a human. It certainly felt very heavy at first, like wearing layers and layers of clothes, and I missed having wings. It wasn't too bad when I was very young, because I had lots of time to play outside with my friends: the trees, the fields, the flowers, as well as birds, butterflies, cows, horses, cats, dogs and other creatures—not spiders though; for some reason I was scared of spiders (funny, I didn't used to be afraid of them). I think my eyes crossed because I was trying to look inward, back to the world I had known as a fairy. Sometimes, when I would see a clump of wild daisies, I'd try to reach back into that world.

I loved those long days of summer—running, climbing, weaving forts out of tall field grasses, and sitting by the lake (this is still, always calming). I liked being outside more than in, because my parents were always worried about something. I didn't pay too much attention, but I did hear some talk about "not having enough money" and concern about "money for food", or "money for presents" at Christmas time. My human parents worked very hard but not with pleasure. This is extraordinarily strange to me! Flower fairies never worry about being fed and their work is always a joy. Beauty and Love intended the world to be like this, not the way most humans experience it: as a life sentence of hard labour, with a reward after death, or in retirement, if they're not too old to enjoy it. Anyway, those long, fun-filled days of dreaming, creating, and imagining soon were cut short. I was sent to prison! They called it "school".

School for flower fairies means being out in the fields with daisies of all ages, and other kinds of plants, flowers, and animals, learning about All-That-Is and our part in the play of Beauty and Love. School for humans means sitting at a desk all day, not moving much, and being quiet. I couldn't even sing or dance when I wanted to, let alone speak! Then I had to learn all this *stuff*! It's not that I wasn't proud when I learned how to read and write; I was. It was fun to do it, but it wasn't fun learning it. They made it hard. And then they did all this comparing, like who's faster, better, or smarter. Wow! I could hardly find a place to stand in all of this and still have trouble with it. But truly, the absolute worst part was outside at recess in grades one to three. This was when some of the big boys would knock me down; then my glasses would fall off and they'd laugh and call me names like "four-eyes" and "goggle-puss". Twice, they actually stomped on my glasses and broke them. This they found even funnier. I don't really understand humans. How do they get to this point of hating each other and hurting each other? Love and Beauty never intended it to be like this. This isn't to say that fairies never get into fights, or play tricks on each other from time to time, we do. But living close to the knowledge of the One brings us back faster and helps us make better choices.

Trying to reach back to the Fairy Realms

What I'm realizing is that, as a human, everything I say (or even think) about another person affects that person, and it affects me as well. So if it's something positive, it builds us up, and if it's negative, it knocks us down on subtle levels. So there's a big responsibility in what I think and say.

As a flower fairy, I often played with *the natural people*—people who live close to the earth, just like fairies. One of them, a young warrior, told me that if I ever needed him for anything, he'd be by my side. So I called to him across time and pretty soon he came and said that he'd stay near me for as long as I needed him. This helped a lot, because though my fairy nature was sturdy, it was delicate as well and his native strength protected me. Luckily, I had my eyes operated on successfully when I was nine. So the bullying has stopped and I no longer need him near me.

Chapter Three

"Seeing"

There is a beautiful creature living
In a hole you have
dug,

so at night I set fruit and grains and little pots of wine and milk
beside your earthen
mounds,

and I often sing to you,
but still, my dear, you do not come out.

I have fallen in love with someone
who is hiding inside
of you.

We should talk about this problem,
otherwise I will never
leave you
alone!

—Hafiz (c. 1320-1389, tr. Ladinsky)

Be loving to the earth. Sow seeds of love on the earth.
The question is not for you to enter into some paradise in the skies.
On the contrary, the question is how to trans-
form this earth into paradise.

'Osho'

The earth is beautiful.
If you start living its beauty, enjoying its joys with
no guilt in your heart, you are in paradise.
If you condemn everything, every small joy, if
you become a condemner, a poisoner,
then the same earth turns into a hell – only for you.

'Osho'

I really miss being part of a big fairy family. My human mother left home at a young age and wasn't close to her family. Her mother died when my mom was only a year old. So she was passed around from relative to relative, until her father re-married when she was seven. At that point, she went back to live with her dad and new stepmother. After this, many babies were born—eight of them, although two died. And she, being the eldest, had to help. She just wanted to get away from it all as fast as she could. So my human family really doesn't know my mom's family, and her dad and stepmother died before I was born

My father's family lives a bit of a distance away from us, so we don't see them often either. But they do include us at family events like Christmas dinners and weddings and such. My dad's mother (my grandmother) can see the *real me*! She never says anything, but I can see it in her eyes: She knows who I really am. She sees Beauty in me and even saw it before my eyes were straightened, and that really helped a lot. My parents' life centers around church activities, so this gives me the equivalent of a large extended family. I like that too! I have an older sister, but we are not close and rarely play together. I do, however, look up to her a lot.

My father is very special to me as well, because he really loves flowers and spends most of his free time (in the warm months) gardening. He plants almost every kind of flower that can grow in our climate. Several times when I was younger, maybe six or seven, my dad and I shared magical, mystical experiences in the garden. Dad would be digging, and I would be weeding beside him. Then it would happen:

Everything became One! I knew that he felt it too, because when I'd look at him, we'd both have tears in our eyes.

As a flower fairy, I lived every moment with the knowledge that everything is connected—that everything is part of *one whole.* But most humans have never had this experience of *Oneness* and simply don't know, so they don't know they are *whole*; they don't know they are Beauty; and they don't know they are Love! I guess this is why they fight so much and kill each other. They don't realize that they are killing parts of themselves. If they knew that "All-That-Is" is, in fact, their very own self, maybe they would stop the killing. If they knew that the planets, stars, earth, air, and even stones, as well as the water, plants, and animals are their *very own body,* perhaps they would treat everything differently. Perhaps they'd treat themselves differently.

When I'm doing things, I notice that, if I am relaxed and in the mind-space that I lived in as a fairy, I can sense my own *true self,* the deepest part of me—the part that is connected to All-That-Is. It's here, talking to me, guiding me gently and lovingly helping me accomplish whatever it is I am doing. It sends me information from the **ground-of-being* (the source of all True Knowledge and Creativity). As a fairy, I lived in this kind of mind-set all the time, communicating intuitively and sensing how things were and what was needed. Now, as a human, I seem to have ways of getting out of harmony, out of sync. There is this other way of being that takes things apart, divides, and separates things. It makes straight lines rather than circles and swirls. It has its purpose, but it can really throw things off 'kilter". It can make everything very tight, with no wiggle room and no space for Spirit to enter.

This is all about *relationship,* not with a "person" really, but with a *presence.* Perhaps it's just a feeling you have in your body and you know it's there. Fairies live in harmony with this, it's what we call **resonance* with All-That-Is.

When I asked the Queen of the Fairies if I could become human, she cautioned me about telling too much, because, as she said, "Humans have a very hard time accepting things they can't quantify." I wasn't sure what she meant by this, but I think I'm starting to understand now.

Humans don't teach children to develop their *reflective, intuitive,* and *creative abilities* very much—hardly at all actually. They focus more on the intellect and acquiring information, not realizing that all they want to know is waiting to be discovered and to reveal itself to them! They sometimes can't see the elephant-in-the-room, so to speak, or they refuse to. They have a great need to control everything, not knowing that while they have the capacity to affect everything (and they do affect everything), they don't ultimately control anything. There is always a larger unfolding pattern at play—literally, at play! There are more layers and levels to life than humans will ever be able to understand. But I can tell you that all you've been told by those humans who have mastered "The Way" (the pure knowledge, not the stuff that has been added on by humans who wish to control others) is true!

There are many, many wonderful, extraordinary humans, and I've met a lot of them. They are kind, caring, loving, giving, and playful. And they can help you to feel very much better when you are sad. I've also met others who came here from the fairy realms (more than you might imagine). Lots of people work hard to improve things for others and to help heal the earth.

See, now here *I* am comparing. It is human nature to do this. Those who live in the seemingly "unmanifest" reality see the world and All-That-Is as one continuous, seamless whole; whereas humans only see parts. That's what happens when something comes into being on earth (the densest layer of manifestation). It can no longer "see" the other layers very well, if at all. It's all about *seeing*! Now if humans use a microscope, or telescope, or other kinds of instruments that they have developed to enhance their seeing, then they can also see other realms, or layers, that they didn't previously know existed. In fact, if you were out in deep space, the earth would be invisible! Electricity was here before humans discovered it, and so were energy, magnetism, and gravity. The invisible world is really not about creating; it is about uncovering; although, we can work with "All-That-Is" to co-create. So other layers can (or do) exist; they just aren't easily seen. It's kind of like water: It can exist as a fluid or as a solid, which we can easily see, or it can exist as moisture, which we can only see when conditions are right—like in the case of droplets on cold windows. Another good example is a garden in winter: It seems to be dead and gone, but in spring, when the conditions are right, it magically reappears in all its splendor. This may be why I had one eye turned in when I was a toddler. It was looking inward while my other eye was looking outward, but weakly. It was as if I were looking back to the *seamless reality* and only weakly outwards towards the denser layers. But I soon realized it didn't work. I felt this deep yearning and longing for *wholeness*, for a connection—to feel a part of something bigger than myself. Now I feel a lot of sadness, especially when I see what is happening to Beauty and Love in this world. I have so many feelings that I'm not used to feeling, at least not this intensely.

The Seamless World

Chapter Four

"Layers"

And yet, though we strain
against the deadening grip
of daily necessity,
I sense there is this Mystery:
All life is being lived.

Who is living it then?
Is it the things themselves,
or something waiting inside them,
like an unplayed melody in a flute?
Is it flowers

Interweaving their fragrances
Or streets, as they wind through time?
Is it animals, moving warmly,
Or the birds, that suddenly rise up?
Who lives it, then? God are you the one
Who is living life?

Rainer Maria Rilke

As a human child, I was very creative. I loved to sing, dance, and paint, and I had a fantastic imagination. I was chock-full of ideas. Even my best friend's grandmother saw this when she visited from time to time. She told my mother not to squash me too much. But my mom had had a lot of her own young self squashed by her overly strict father, and by too many demands and responsibilities placed on her at too young an age. Remember, she had lost her mom when she was only a year old. So she practised what she had learned. She made life much too much about work and duty and not enough about *creativity, spontaneity* and *fun*. She had a wonderful singing voice, and as a single woman, had acted in musicals and had a small radio show. Later as a wife and mother, she performed solos at church, sang in the choir, and still acted in amateur theatre, but duty left her very little time to really pursue any of this.

Basically, all of my daisy flower fairy qualities got squeezed into a small dark corner (very like the corner behind the furnace in the basement where I went to hide when I was feeling unloved and unlovable) and they were only let out for brief times. Even these became more infrequent as I grew up, fell in love, married, and started a family of my own. There didn't seem to be a place in this world for what I saw back then. There certainly wasn't anyone to talk to about it.

Luckily, my husband had some elf-like qualities, which showed in his love of Nature and his *gentle creative soul*. He worked in a *creative field* and really loved music. He helped to remind me of my connection to the earth and all the Natural

World, because I had really gotten very far away from it in my daily life as a teenager and young adult.

Although I was naturally very *Spiritual, as I aged, I felt that I had become covered over with these layers and layers of, what I called "programming". I was eager to go to church and learn about Spiritual things but then found that it was mostly people repeating information about other people's *spiritual experiences*, without having had an experience themselves. This tended to take me away from my *inner world* and the *teacher within*. If we are indeed all one, I must learn to listen to the *One within* and not the many without. However, from time to time, I did hear the *One* speaking through others.

Another source of heaviness in the human experience seems to come from the accumulation of trace memories from all of our many ancestors. All the joys and sorrows, all the feuds, wars, losses, pain, suffering, and hurts, as well as the achievements, are carried from generation to generation. It's rather like the way earth and stones are made up of layers of broken rock, sand, dust, vegetation, human and animal bones, and waste materials, layer upon layer for eons, which then carry the memories and history of the planet. It is this that science now examines with carbon dating and DNA tests, to learn more about the earth's history. We also pick up some of this information through our food, which is grown in the soil, and the minerals that are absorbed into our body through the water we drink. As well, we tend to hold in our feelings, hoarding them at times. This all weighs us down and interferes with our ability to realize our *true nature*, which is Light and Energy.

Can I learn to see through the darkness and heaviness to the *light at the center*? Can I learn to be it, live it, and reflect it to others? Can I see that we are all in this together—the humans, the animals, the plants, the earth, the air, the water, the living planet, and the entire cosmos? Right now, this is the next great challenge for humanity to overcome, before we make ourselves extinct. I see now that countries also exhibit this heaviness, born of the past actions of our ancestors, or invading peoples. They too, can become bogged down with pain, sorrow, hatred, aggression, and greed.

I began feeling heavier and heavier, and living far more in my head than connected to the rest of my body, intuition and the Natural World. Emotions can also make us feel heavy, unless we work at learning how to shift their energy. They are, after all, rather like weather systems—discordant energies that need space to spin outward and to dissipate. I was not accustomed to having to deal with so many different emotions and with such intensity, at times. In fact, I'm still not!

I have found myself drawn to Eastern traditions, which is why, as a young adult, I began to practice (and later teach) yoga and meditation, when most people still thought this kind of thing was pretty foreign and weird. These were great gifts that still help me to stay grounded and connected. But the direct connection through Nature and Creativity somewhat diminished in me back then, until my mid-twenties. The practices of yoga and meditation reminded me of how to feel light in my body, almost as if I could fly again! They reminded me that I am, in fact, not this earthbound body, but an *airy, fairy being*! In fact, each human could benefit from becoming aware of their *airy fairy* self, a self of *wholeness, lightness and magical possibilities!*

There were times when I reconnected, like the year I spent only teaching yoga and doing art. That year has always stood out for me as one of my happiest. It was shortly after this that my husband and I bought a house and started a family.

Our first child was wise beyond her years and very, very *creative.* I encouraged this and did a lot of arts and crafts activities with her, but I only sporadically gave myself to my own creations, just fitting them in and around other things that seemed more pressing. I followed well my mother's teachings of hard work and duty. I did, however, make a promise to myself that one day I'd give my Creativity the time and attention it deserved. Meanwhile, years passed, another child was born, and he had a sensitive and *creative nature* too, which I nourished in him as well. I loved being a mother; it gave me time to be in Nature again and to be *spontaneous* and *creative.* In the summer months, I made sure my children spent lots of time in Nature and roaming free in a Natural Environment. This is where the greatest learning takes place, as Nature and the Wilderness are skilled teachers. You might ask how this can be, but if you've spent a lot of time in the Natural World you'll know what I mean. These lessons are subtle, like the one on the *cycles of life* that include both birth and death, or the one on opposites and how they co-exist. And there are loads of lessons about Beauty. I also learned a lot about Love from Nature and (of course) how to come into *stillness* and to *center.*

When both children were in school, I decided to return to school myself. Now fairies, only study and learn from direct experience—by observing and doing. All the book learning and lectures made my head hurt and disconnected me even further from my body. Thank goodness I kept practicing yoga and meditation. This helped! My first yoga teacher had also taught me a valuable lesson when she said, "Take what's here for you and leave the rest." This Wisdom has allowed me to stay open to everything, and to get what is helpful for me, instead of shutting down when things aren't packaged in a certain way or don't meet my expectations.

At times, I find it hard navigating in the world that humans have created. Everything is so separate and sped up. Humans have a way of dividing everything, often with straight lines that form squares, or rectangles, so that (metaphorically) we bump up against walls or get trapped in corners. I sometimes find myself doing this in my mind and then imposing it on the outside world, which (in fact) does not have private properties, borders, countries, or other such divisions. Sometimes I think it is our attempt to create permanence and stability in an ever-changing and unpredictable world. It's a delusion, thinking that we have power and control over Nature.

I watch how the Natural World is being taken over by moneymaking endeavours that are squeezing the wild animals more and more into preserves, parks, and sanctuaries. This has greatly reduced their numbers, because they can no longer roam freely and hunt as they used to and it has interfered with their migratory routes. Wilderness itself is being shrunk through our ignorance of the enormous positive effects it has on us. These are areas that can *hold the center* for us, in addition to their particular cleansing and life-giving qualities. What we don't realize is that plants and animals are *highly intelligent, sensitive, and intuitive beings.* They are naturally very *loving* and *compassionate* and we are only just starting to discover how they can heal us of many ills. We can learn to communicate with them and know them as *great allies,* just as the people-who-live-close-to-the-earth do.

We are destroying the world's natural forests, not understanding that trees are *great beings* and the lungs of our planet—and therefore our lungs, as well. Humans share 50% of their DNA with trees. There is only *One Breath.*

We are interrupting the flow of great rivers and lakes, not understanding that they are the circulatory system of the earth's body and therefore of our bodies too. Unaware of the complex connections between various waterways, we are wreaking great havoc! For example, the destruction of wetlands affects our oceans and myriad life forms that interact with so many other systems in the great balance of life on this planet... and on and on.

Many of the people-who-live-close-to-the-earth, have also been reduced to living in territories and reserves, no longer able to live off the land, which they are so *intricately and spiritually connected to.* This, together with their experiences at residential school, has affected their *souls,* and many have become *dispirited.* Thank goodness some have worked hard to raise themselves back up and rebuild what their ancestors had in the past. This has been necessary in order for them to have a foundation on which to build for the future.

Of late, I have been aware of how I can put things into little boxes in my mind and then see the *wholeness* of the world all broken into little bits. When I studied at the university, I noticed that all the subjects were separate, each with its own department, each not knowing what the other was doing. There was little, or no collaboration, or communication. Even within faculties, like the different sciences or the different arts, there was little or no contact. Fairies tend to work in groups, more like swarms, so it's hard to understand all this working alone. In swarms, it takes less individual energy, because the whole is greater than the sum of its parts. Have you ever watched a murmuration of starlings, or a school of fish? They move as one body, as if they had one brain. There's more *creativity* and a greater ability to receive information from All-That-Is in a swarm or group.

Funny! Scientists and artists of all kinds are not that far apart, if they are the sort who look and listen deeply.... sitting with things, moving up close, then stepping back, thinking divergently, and following their *intuition.* I see that these people open the door to working *with wisdom* and *the way things are.* They have often discovered the magic of using their *creative imagination.* Little boxes are not bad, as long as there is a movement back to the whole, to understand the way things fit together and connect and ultimately become greater than the sum of the parts. I'm working hard to re-learn this. For example, take the negative space in a painting—the so-called "empty space" between the people, or objects, in the picture. These areas are as important to the whole of the picture as any subject matter; they are integral to the whole design. Just as they are joined together in *one whole* called "a picture", so too is All-That-Is.

It has been less than a hundred years since scientists began to explore the infinitesimally small (what they call quantum mechanics) and to uncover the world that has always existed at that level—what, as fairies, we used to call the **ground of being.* Some scientists are now realizing that the scientific realities they are seeing, at this level, verify what many wise and intuitive men and woman (mystics, healers, spiritual masters) have known for two thousand years!

The more deeply I explore the human body, the more I see how complex it truly is. There are systems within systems, all interconnected in a delicate balance. We are not machines! And our bodies are *energetically and intuitively* connected with other bodies and to the Natural World around us. We are shaped by, and in turn shape, everything we come in contact with.

Life on this planet is not a black and white proposition, it is about shades of grey, or a continuum. One area where this error is most noticeable is the failure to realize that we, as humans, live on different levels, for example, the physical, the mental/emotional, and the ethereal. These can be thought of as equivalent to ice, water and steam. Now it's easy to see how the latter are "not one, not two". This means, that even though we make a distinction, there really isn't one *at some level.* Many, many times I've been in groups where a topic is being discussed without acknowledgement of the various levels, or forms, of the subject under discussion. This leads to misunderstandings and discussions that go nowhere, or that are at cross-purposes. It is very hard to realize the interpenetration of all things. For example, a chair appears to be a solid, physical object and yet, on closer inspection, science has revealed it's deeper nature, that of atoms moving about slowly. Then quantum mechanics, reveals a still deeper reality. Therefore, we need to clarify at what level we are speaking, while at the same time, remembering that all are One and One is all!

Just as the dark, fecund underworld brings forth the gardens in spring, so too does my own *inner darkness* bear seeds of *creativity*. And what's more, the seeming void of death is but the very *ground of our being*, holding us in loving arms and supporting us constantly through all of our travails. Death is but a part of the cycle of life; birth is its opposite. The furthest, deepest, darkest reaches of the cosmos is the birthing place—the very womb of All-That-Is. Even in so-called outer space, there are dimensions of beings watching over us constantly, from celestial angels to great souls who have learned the ways of navigating and evolving and now work to help us evolve too, before we do ourselves in! Much time has passed and I have had many more lessons on this journey of learning to be human.

The Guardians of the Earth

The fairy realms are much closer to *wholeness*, to the *eternal*, and so time doesn't really exist for us and neither does death as humans experience it. While my children were still quite young, my husband was diagnosed with cancer and died just two short years later. His death shattered the world we had built around us. It caused me to dig down very deeply into the *ground of my being* and taught me many lessons. His dying also gave me a peek behind "the veil". This tragedy was followed closely by the deaths of many who were dear to me: parents, in-laws, aunts, uncles, and a few treasured friends. These losses had the effect of peeling layers off of me. They opened me up to much deeper levels of my *inner being*. I began getting images and poems—lots of them. It was like a great river flowing out of me. This was a very new experience for me. One of the first poems I received spoke deeply to my experience at that time. I had had a dream of a great storm, with lots of wind that had literally blown in a window in a gymnasium, leaving broken glass all over the floor. In the dream I entered the room, and horrified by the destruction, I started to hold fragments of glass up to the light and I became fascinated with their Beauty and how the light was refracted in these shards. Within days of having had this dream, I received this poem, called "You Feel Shattered".

My writings and drawings were teaching me to "trust the process" and they were healing me. I can still access this *river of wisdom* and *creativity*.

I also realize that souls can work together in soul groups, be they family or friends, to help each other evolve. Occasionally, a great soul can evolve alone, such as the Buddha, or other wise beings (like shamans, medicine people and mystics), but most people need a collective to really pull in the higher energies from All-That-Is, *the ground of being*, in order to evolve.

You feel s h a t t e r e d......
All the pieces
of your life
like so much
broken glass.
Broken dreams,
shards of relationships,
the shrapnel of many wars.
Struggle
Hope
Try
Fall..............
short or,
be blown a p a r t
TRUST!
..........what??

Come,
let me show you
how to take these
broken bits
and fashion them
into a new creation
a n e w pa tte r n
It's the Process............

TRUST THE PROCESS!

I don't know too much about how this works, but I have seen it in action when the suffering of one family member causes other members to grow and heal. In great tragedies when many lives are sacrificed, it can raise the level of consciousness of vast groups of people and bring out the very best in humans.

The Stained-glass Window of My Life (...a work in progress)

For some souls, dying can be their *healing journey*; for others, healing while in their physical body is the journey. People who die can also aid and quicken the evolutionary process for the living, through the very process of their dying. Sometimes we can sense that people on the other side are helping us.

My mother had programmed me to believe that "we are not here for ourselves but to help others", so my career as a therapist really gave me lots of opportunities to be present for others. My work permitted me to walk with others through difficult times, sharing with them skillful means to navigate the turbulent waters, deep forests, desert places, and foreign lands in the inner landscape of their lives. This, too, taught me to see through the layers to the place where we are *all one being* and how we can learn to *stay centered* in ourselves in *the-place-that-remains-untouched* by all the passing show. I see very clearly now how the layers of civilization, "shoulds", and little boxes can keep us earth-bound, head-centered, and heavy.

Meanwhile, the promise to pay attention to my *creativity* and give it time and space, kept getting further and further away. Of course, I still have a lot to do to release my mother's teachings of duty and hard work. I have had to work on *forgiveness*, especially regarding my parents. I had to learn to see beyond their human selves to the *essence* that was being carried in them, and that it had its part to play in the *great creation* of All-That-Is. I see now that my father's weaknesses, which let me down at times, also taught me gentleness, patience, and love, especially for the Natural World. My mother's ferocity forced me to be strong, and demonstrated to me a faith-in-action and a stick-to-it-ness although it has often squashed me. Fortunately, my sister and I became very close as the years pass.

I have tried really hard to be a good human being, and to live up to all the expectations that my parents, society, church, school, and I, myself, had placed on me, always promising that one day I'd give myself fully to this *river of creativity*. Oh, I was *creative* in the way I worked and helped many to connect with their *bodies* and their *deepest selves*, but I always felt this sadness and emptiness, as if something was missing. For me, Nature was a model for both a masculine and feminine parent: Strong, Wise, Loving, Giving, Comforting, Gentle, Creative, Forgiving, Compassionate, and Patient—qualities my parents were often not able to model for me because of their own woundings and programming. I learned to feel *great compassion* for them and to see the *essence of who they truly were* and the gifts they had to offer to the world.

Basically, I've been trying to navigate in this world of duality. I guess a non-dual world might be flat, dull and boring, but it is possible to have it both ways: Not one, not two. The way through, I'm discovering, is *to hold the center*. By this I mean *staying centered in your heart*, and not allowing the pairs of opposites to pull you one way or the other, tossing you about—good-bad, right-wrong, and so on. When I'm able to stay *heart-centered*, to *dwell in my heart space*, fully feeling, but not judging, or choosing one over the other, a portal opens and another way is perceived. So, for example, there are many violent and tragic things happening in the world around us these days. I don't need to list them, we are all only too aware of them. In the face of these events, we have a choice of how to respond. We can be overcome by fear, or hatred, and then perpetuate more of the same in the world, or we can become divided and say these people are right and these are wrong without truly standing in their shoes and seeing things through their eyes, or we can explore a third option: we *can connect with the place in our body that is at the center* and *breathe into the spaciousness* that can be felt there. As we do this, we can feel our body relax and create even more space within. Letting go of all thoughts, ideas, and concepts, we can just *be in this spaciousness, holding this center where all is one* in the midst of the chaos, and returning again and again to our breath. In simply doing this, we affirm our *ethereal nature,* aligning ourselves with All-That-Is. At this level, all truly is "possibility" (as quantum mechanics has shown us) so we can hold this space and wait for things to shift. The *great pattern* is unfolding if we can learn to "trust the process". This also allows us to *connect with deep wisdom* and the *heart,* and in doing so we are more likely to take "right action" and be in "right relationship", free from personal agendas. To be able to hear our *inner voice* we need times of quiet. All enlightened masters, shamans, mystics, yogis, etc., have learned how to do this—to open to *a larger field of reality* and to navigate there. I believe we are all gifted with the ability to learn to do this. So all experiences can be seen as opportunities, or trainings, in learning to *hold-the-center* and *open-the-portal.* I'm working on this!

Chapter Five

"Decisions"

Awake awhile.
It does not have to be
Forever,
Right now.

One step upon the Sky's soft skirt
Would be enough.

Hafiz,
Awake awhile.
Just one true moment of Love
Will last for days.

Rest all your elaborate plans and tactics
For knowing Him,
For they are all just frozen buds
Far,
So far from Summer's Divine Gold.

Awake, my dear.
Be kind to your sleeping heart.
Take it out into the vast fields of Light
And let it breathe.

Say,
"Love,
Give me back my wings.
Lift me nearer."
Say to the sun and moon,
Say to our dear Friend,
"I will take You up now, Beloved,
On that wonderful Dance you promised."

—Hafiz (c. 1320-1389, tr. Ladinsky)

A flower fairy's life is a lot less complicated, living as they do, with Beauty and Love all of the time. A fairy's only duty is to take care of the garden, the plants, the trees, and the animals, and to co-create gardens together with All-That-Is, as well as with other elementals and humans. Some humans think they do this alone, unaware that the fairies are hard at work to bring Beauty, Harmony, and Love to every corner of the world. They just live *their true nature, their essence,* all the time, shining their light and enhancing the wellbeing of All-That-Is.

What has taken me a long time to realize, as a human, is that when I consciously root myself in *my true reality,* my *true self,* which is the *ground-of-being* of All-That-Is, then life unfolds and consciousness expands. It is here that the *life-giving power* of All-That-Is can expand and unfold in me in a *natural way.* When I am focused only on my own small worldview, and, in fact, struggling against the larger unfolding picture, I block life. I block what naturally wants to unfold through me. I go against the flow and this creates dis-ease that can eventually lead to illness, violence, and destruction in the world. This happens when enough people get wedded to a negative perspective, or intent—for example, hatred towards a specific group. This is to be caught in the web of duality and to fail to see the gradation in everything from one extreme to the other.

Authentic power comes from aligning my *intentions* with the highest: Love, Beauty, Harmony, Creativity, Compassion, Forgiveness, Joy, and Justice. It is these qualities that naturally flow through us when we *hold the center* and *come into resonance* with All-That-Is. This is what Wilderness and the Natural World can teach us: How to do this, just by its very *presence* and *rootedness*. This is why it is so important to get out of the energies of city life and into the country, or better still, the wild places. In these settings, the *energies* and *presence* of All-That-Is are so concentrated that they can help us connect to the *ground of being* more easily. Just seeing the grandeur of the sky unobstructed, or feeling the magnificence and steadfastness of mountains, awakens evolutionary codes in our *being*. We need only remove the obstacles (such as busyness, distraction, living only in our heads, lack of presence, blocked emotions, not letting go of the past, preoccupation with fear, greed, hatred, jealousy, envy, desire for *power over* versus *power with*, addictions, and the like) and come into the present moment. No small task really!

I understand better now how to listen to my *inner wisdom*, to pay attention to subtle promptings and to give less importance to the "programming". The teachings I received from my parents, school, church and society were supposed to point me in the right direction, which they did at times, but they actually pointed me away from my Inner Wisdom, especially the teachings that were tied up with punishment, guilt, and competition. I now know that Wisdom's ways are only about Beauty and Love and these manifest in people as Patience, Kindness, Peace, Calm, Justice, Compassion, and so on.

I had totally forgotten the fact that, when I chose to become human, I had asked to experience as many emotions as possible. How very naive I was! But now I can see that the events of my life have allowed me to discover the array of colours that are my emotions and how all the opposites create each other, joy and sorrow, for example. Once, during my husband's dying process, I was experiencing incredibly intense pain and sorrow as I watched him lying there. Then I turned to look out the hospital window and saw the most beautiful sunset that I had ever seen and was suddenly filled with immense joy such as I had never known. Turning back to him, my joy turned once again to pain and sorrow. This taught me the relationship between these two seeming opposites, and how I could not have known the depth of one without the other.

I've learned that, when things fall apart, there is greater potential for change and growth. Walking a labyrinth taught me that, just when I think I am nearing the center, I may be thrown back to the outer circle. And there, as feelings of discouragement, even despair, arise, I can keep walking and suddenly find myself home, at the center! These *life lessons* are teaching me to more skillfully deal with the human condition.

Some souls find each other across time and the *turnings of life.* I have re-married now, somehow finding my young fairy self's friend, the native warrior, embodied again as a man! He still has my back! He, like my first husband, shares my deep love of Nature and understands my awareness of *spiritual realities.* He too loves music.

But it has taken me many, many years to realize my True Self. My flower fairy nature has helped me with this, because I finally came to "see" that doing what I most love -—writing poems and stories, painting, dancing, singing, and giving free rein to my Creativity—is how I feel happiest and full, instead of sad, empty, and crabby. I've tried being good, tried being dutiful, tried pleasing everyone else at the expense of pleasing myself. These are very human practices I've discovered. I followed all the rules as I saw them, and worked hard to help others. This is not to say that all of this rule-keeping was wrong, of course. Love and Beauty use everything to weave things together for good. I was fulfilling my destiny, but I very nearly by-passed just being myself! Now, I'm realizing that, in expressing my Creativity, and being myself—my deepest fairy nature, my *essence*—along with giving this self as a gift to the world, I am living *my true purpose* my highest calling.

For years I struggled with old beliefs, like that "spending time creating or sharing creative thoughts and works with others is selfish!" (It isn't selfish when others do this; it is only selfish when I do it). But slowly, very slowly, a new day is dawning and this day, and the next are being filled with the making of wonder-filled things, poems, books, paintings, and more, all born from the union of Love and Beauty. And I will know that my purpose has been accomplished, which is to bring my *fairy magic* into human form for the enhancement and pleasure of All-That-Is.

You see, as I said earlier, in the fairy realms everything is seamless—*one whole*. Fairies live in this reality all of the time. As a human, I now live in denser layers of manifestation than the "invisible world" (which I call the *not-yet-visible-world*) in which I lived in as a fairy. Yet I'm learning that I have, in my nature, the ability to choose what I relate to and see. I can learn to see through the layers—layers that have been created over time and then passed on from generation to generation, layers that are made of "habits of seeing", conventions, and heady ideas about reality, instead of *experiencing for myself, being present in the moment,* relating to what is happening now, and "truly seeing". I can choose to see Wholeness, Beauty, and Love, or not. And depending on what I see, I create the world I live in. Do I want to live in the world of the past, recreating over and over old hurtful patterns, or do I want to stay *present in the now, feeling into the moment, and listening to deep wisdom?*

If I could only fully realize just how open to change everything truly is. It can change in a blink of an eye when I let go of rigid and negative thoughts. Even in the toughest of times —particularly in the toughest of times—there are many blessings and always light at the center. I know this even when I don't always see it. This Light is a still flame and many guard its gates.

The Keepers of the Flame

I realize this is a very unique time to be present on the earth. No other humans have had the opportunity to see the whole planet from another perspective, but the astronauts have given our common brain this vision and thereby have watered the seeds of our common humanity—a vision of *one united world.* I know deep down we all have within ourselves, a place that yearns for *wholeness, peace, and joy.*

I see now, that I have a choice and that on the next *turning of life* there will be no separation. I will consciously choose to allow *essence* to be born on earth through me in human form, so the work of Love and Beauty can continue on all levels and layers. I know now, in this body, that I have the capacity to function on many levels at once. It may be on the physical, concrete, practical level, or on a metaphysical level, going outside the boundaries of the physical body and using *intuition* and *conscious intent* to effect change for the good. The *great secret* is that we *all have wings!* We can rise up when weighed down. If I can choose to consciously evolve myself, letting out more of my *fairy essence,* then, I will further the work of All-That-Is. We are in a constant dance and relationship, because we are a part of the fabric of All-That-Is, and this is to *be alive, loving, creative and playful!* I am choosing to *see* the Eternal One in all sentient beings, to live my *winged nature,* and to free myself from the weight of those layers. The conditions are right, now, for me to *lighten up*!

What do you choose?

Postscript

No one lives his life.
Disguised since childhood,
Haphazardly assembled
from voices and fears and little pleasures,
we come of age as masks.

Our true face never speaks.
Rainer Maria Rilke

"Through pride we are ever deceiving ourselves. But deep down
below the surface of the average conscience
a still, small voice says to us,
Something is out of tune."
C.G. Jung

"Inside you
there's an artist you don't know about…"

Rumi

I can't imagine what you the reader must be thinking at this point, but I can tell you what I thought after this story was written down. The very first thing was that it "wore my clothes". By this I mean that the fairy is wearing the very fabric of my life. Her story is my story! Of course I reflected a lot on this ... Am I, actually a fairy living a human experience?

I was not a child that "saw" fairies, but I often thought that I felt them around, and I was the kind of dreamy, creative, imaginative child who loved nature and being out-of-doors. I remember playing at the very back of our half-acre property, where there were tall trees and a sort of grassy area where lily-of-the-valley grew in profusion every spring. I'd dance around and sing to the trees and flowers and perhaps the fairies. I felt very, very connected to the natural world and did have several profound "spiritual experiences" when I was between six and eight years of age. While some might say, "How could you remember them?" I have since had several confirmations of these times. My dad was present in the garden with me when they happened, and although we never spoke of it, I knew that he had had a similar experience. Then, when I was forty years old, I had the same experience—this time with my seven or eight-year-old daughter. Again, it took place in nature, and as had happened with my dad, we both had tears in our eyes, so I knew that she had felt what I had felt. Later it happened again with my second husband-to-be. It was then that I asked my dad if he remembered these happenings from my childhood and he nodded knowingly, being no longer able to speak due to a stroke.

Am I a fairy? To be honest, I don't truly know. There is this very big part of me who is wiser than the self I ordinarily relate to and she's very creative. Field daisies have always been my favourite flowers. I even chose them for my bridal bouquet. That part of me loves the natural world (well actually all of me loves the natural world) and she really wants a lot more space and control over how I live my life. She's very tired of being shoved to the back burner, so-to-speak, and she wishes to spend her remaining years painting, writing, gardening, and enjoying the natural world by camping, kayaking, hiking, biking, and through making and sharing her creative projects. Strange, this is exactly what I want as well! I have always been aware of this part of me but not as a fairy part of me. Looking at my life through this lens has become a very interesting and enlightening experience. Since writing this book I see that the makings of it have been coming through me for a long time. I see a process that has been unfolding in my life over many, many years and the threads that I have been following—not knowing where they would lead me. Recently, I can see how I adopted a "warrior stance" after having been bullied at age six. This was a way of protecting the fragile-yet-strong, delicate part of me. I see that I hid her away by adopting an attitude of; "the best defense is a strong offense". It's time to own this and let go of it now. I don't have it all figured out by any means, but I am beginning to understand more. It's rather unnerving really!

Recently, I recalled an experience I had had back in my thirties, while attending a ten-day spiritual retreat at my favourite yoga center in Massachusetts. We were doing an experiential process about discovering our symbol for healing. At the end of the guided imaging, we were instructed to lower our heads, eyes closed, and then to open our eyes while looking at our feet. What did we see? I saw big, black, furry, panther paws! On my right a young native warrior was standing, and on my left there was a flower fairy lying on the ground. She seemed weak. The message I received was that, when the fairy was strong enough to take her place, the circle would be complete and I would come into my healing panther power. Maybe, by publishing this book, my inner fairy self can stand up and take her place in the circle. I promise I'll let you know if my healing panther power comes into being!

Strange as all this may seem, I choose to believe that we all have parts of ourselves that want to be expressed, and to "lighten up" or be "enlightened". We all have wings that can lift us up in the darkest of times and help us see a bigger world, a deeper reality—one that interpenetrates the visible world and the *not-yet-visible world.* The fairy represents the spiritual part of me, which is far lighter, more ethereal, and wiser than the "me" that was created by my history and *programming.* Just as she wants to be fully born in me, so does Spirit want to awaken in the physical reality *as* me, or *you.* This is our journey and perhaps has always been mankind's journey. The German poet Rainer Maria Rilke wrote:

"...For the god
Wants to know himself in you."

Right now I'm reading Carl Jung's *Red Book*—a beautifully illustrated copy of a series of journals he kept. These describe very real encounters he had while intentionally journeying around in his unconscious. It was out of this rich world of archetypal figures, the dead, the sacred and the profane that he formulated his basic ideas and concepts as a psychologist, back in the earliest days of the new field of psychology. This book was only published about six years ago, although it was written in the early 1900's. Only a handful of people close to Jung knew of its existence. While it is thought by many, to be the pivotal work of one of the era's great thinkers, it has created quite a stir in psychological circles, as it brings into question many long held ideas about therapy, the unconscious, psyche, the imaginal realms, the collective unconscious and so forth. Recently, too, I read a book by psychologist Mary T. Beben called *The Pleiadian House of Initiation*. She, too, avows that all of her experiences are real, not imaginary.

Lastly, I received a message from Dr. Jean Houston, a philosopher and one of the founders of The Human Potential Movement. It was in connection with one of her on-line courses that I had signed up for. She told a story about meeting Albert Einstein when she was eight years old. One of her classmates asked how he could get to be as smart as Mr. Einstein was, and he replied that they should "read fairy tales". When another student asked a similar question, Mr. Einstein replied, "read more fairy tales!" As an adult, she understood better what he had meant—that they should grow their imaginations and that it is from the imaginal realm that the most potent ideas come—ones that can change the world. All of these writings have given me courage.

A Fairy's Tale seems to be the continuation of a series of short volumes of poems and drawings called, Soul Journeys. This series began shortly after the death of my mother in 1994. But the foundation for this writing process was born shortly after the death of my husband, seven years earlier in 1987.

One of the methods I used to deal with my husband's death, was painting. I spent two hours at a time, weekly, for six months, at a friend's atelier, just painting furiously with poster paints and newsprint. I'd put the brush in my non-dominant hand to get me out of my head and then I'd let colours choose me and I'd paint quickly. I'd paint from a *felt sense*, meaning some sensation in my body. For example, it might be a heaviness in my chest, or a tight ball in my abdomen. I often would cry through these sessions, not knowing what specifically I was crying about. At the end of two hours I'd feel relatively complete until the next time. Finally, this process came to a natural end when I felt I had faithfully put on paper what I was feeling inside.

However, another strange thing occurred in relation to this painting process. One day, before this process came to completion, I was sitting and taking a break, when a voice in my chest spoke to me. It said, "I'm an artist; I'm an artist, and it's the only thing in the world that matters!" I remember very clearly looking down at my chest and saying, "Well, I'm a psychologist!" I didn't know what this all meant, and frankly I'm only just beginning to understand, but at that time, I did make a promise to the voice to try to find out the meaning.

It wasn't until seven years later, after the deaths of several close friends and many family members, including my mother, that a great stream of images and poetry started to flow and I realized that this outpouring was connected to those painting sessions. The flow has never stopped, although it has ebbed at times. This is usually because I get too busy with other things. It was in 2008 that this flow produced this book and another short story which is fiction. All of these writings have started with a word or an image, and then they just pour out fully formed. I have always felt that they are written by some part of me who is much smarter and wiser than the "me" I know. There truly is more under heaven and earth than we can ever conceive of, so I'll leave the rest up to you.

I remember that seven years ago, I was too afraid to put this story out into the world, but today I feel confident that it will find those readers who need this information now in their lives. I hope it will encourage others in their own explorations with their creative, imaginative selves, so that they can tap into the richness of all the dimensions of life and become more aware of the big picture, of which we are an important part. I'm less afraid now to live all of who I am and to be seen. There is a lot of uncovering going on throughout the world right now. I am trusting this process.

I marvel at how much the world has changed in the intervening years. We are living at a time that requires great courage, steadiness, love, compassion, flexibility, and creativity. As I watched (on TV) the millions of people who gathered in Paris recently, led by a line of world leaders with their arms intertwined, walking in strength and solidarity in spite of racial, political, and religious differences, I felt overwhelmed. I believe this was a glimpse of this "something larger" that is taking shape in the world in the very midst of the chaos and destruction—perhaps even because of it. It is a "something" that does not give into fear, but rather draws us together in strength and courage, and invites us to hold the center, instead of reverting to old patterns that have not worked.

This is a time for discovering our own wisdom, writing down what we know, and sharing it to help others, not to become prophets or the like, not relying on gurus and masters, but finding our own connection to the Source. In this way, we can fit the pieces of the larger pattern together and more skillfully take our place in the great unfolding of Creation. As my Fairy self so aptly puts it, "I'm choosing to lighten up. What *do you* choose?"

End Notes

Pg. 9 ***Manifest,** by this I mean that it becomes visible to the eye. Like a garden in spring, it manifests itself after being "invisible" over the winter.

Pg. 19 ***Resonance**, this term is often used in an acoustic sense, like strings on an instrument vibrating together. Sometimes different drums in a room will start to vibrate with the sound of the one drum being hit, even though they are not being touched. I've read somewhere that heart cells can do the same thing. It is this that I am speaking of here, in relation to human beings, who also can come into resonance with each other by coming into harmony with another's vibration—energy, breath, or heartbeat.

Pg. 18, 31 ***Ground of Being** (Wikipedia) Text is available under the Creative Commons Attribution-ShareAlike License

In Philosophy: The **Ground** or **Urground** ("Original Ground") is the concept of an unconditional reality, which transcends limited, conditional, everyday existence. Eliade defines the Absolute as the Divine Ground (German: *Grund* or *Urgrund*, "Original Ground")

that defies "all possibilities of rational comprehension" and can only be "grasped as a mystery or paradox". John Daniel Dadosky. *The Structure of Religious Knowing: Encountering the Sacred in Eliade and Lonergan.* State University of New York Press, 2004. ISBN 0791460614. P. 66

In Tibetan Buddhism: Dzogchen ***Ground*** is the primordial state. It has been rendered 'Base', 'Basis', 'Ground' and 'Ground of Being'. It is the already self-perfected state of our primordial nature, which needs no 'perfecting', for it has always been perfect from the very beginning, just like the sky. It is uncreated, yet spontaneously accomplished. Rigpa Shedra rigpawiki.org

In Quantum Physics: In quantum field theory, the vacuum state is the quantum state with the lowest possible energy; it contains no physical particles, and is the energy of **the ground state.**

In Theology: Paul Tillich's ontological view of God, different from theological theism, is that it transcends it by being the foundation or ultimate reality that "precedes" all beings. God is **the ground** upon which all beings exist. We cannot perceive God as an object, which is related to a subject, because God *precedes* the subject-object dichotomy. Paul Tillich (1959), *Theology of Culture,* Oxford University Press, ISBN 978-0-19976353-5. p.15

Pg. 26 ***Spiritual:** By this I mean, being aware of, and connected to, the deeper layers of reality other than just the physical world. Sensing, feeling, and connecting with things that may, or may not, appear in physical form, such as inner promptings, the sense of a tree as a spiritual being, experiences of the Wholeness of everything in Nature. It does not have to do with religion per se, although the world's religions are based on an individual's (Jesus, Buddha, Mohammed, for example) spiritual experiences. Someone who views herself as Spiritual accepts that the world is Spiritual, made of Spirit at its deepest levels, and while they may follow the teachings of certain traditions, they have likely had experiences of immanence themselves and do not rely fully on someone else's experience.

Bibliography

Various quotes throughout from C.G. Jung, In *Memories, Dreams, Reflection,* Aniela Jaffé (Editor), Richard and Clara Winston (Translators), Vintage Books Edition, Random House Inc., New York, 1989.

The Guest House, by Rumi, Coleman Barks (translator), *The Essential Rumi,* Harper Collins Pub. 1995. p.109

Chapter I *The Mind of Absolute Trust* Seng-Ts'an (? – 606) In *The Enlightened Heart,* edited by Stephen Mitchell, Harper & Row Pub., N.Y. 1989 Pgs. 26-28

Chapter II "The Way Wings Should", Rumi, (1207 -1273) Daniel Ladinsky (translator). In *Love Poems From God: Twelve Sacred Voices from the East and West,* Penguin USA Inc., New York, 2002. p. 67

Chapter III "Beautiful Creature", Hafiz (1320-1389A.D.) Daniel Ladinsky (translator). *In Love Poems From God:Twelve Sacred Voices from the East and West,* Penguin USA Inc., New York, 2002. p. 174

Osho quotations courtsy of Osho International Foundation, www.osho.com

Chapter IV "Und doch, obwohl ein…/And yet, though we strain…", Rainer Maria Rilke, (1875-1926) In *Rilke's Book of Hours: Love Poems From God,* translated by Anita Barrows and Joanna Macy, Riverhead Books, Penguin USA Inc., New York, 1997. p 167.

Chapter V *"Awake Awhile"* Hafiz (1320 -1389 A.D.*)* In *I Heard God Laughing: Poems of Hope and Joy,* Daniel Ladinsky, (translator), Sufism Reoriented, 1996, Penguin Group (USA), 2006. P. 38

Postscript "Ich bin nur einer deiner…/*No one lives his life*" by Rainer Maria Rilke (1875-1926). In *Rilke's Book of Hours: Love Poems To God* translated by Anita Barrows and Joanna Macy , Riverhead Books, Penguin Group USA Inc., New York, 1997. p.165 "As Once the Winged Energy of Delight….", Rainer Maria Rilke (1875-1926) In *The Enlightened Heart: An Anthology of Sacred Poetry* edited by Stephen Mitchell, Harper & row Pub., N.Y. 1989. Pg. 133 *"Say Yes Quickly", Rumi (1207-1273)* In *The Enlightened Heart: An Anthology of Sacred Poetry,* edited by Stephen Mitchell, Harper & Row Pub., N.Y. 1989. p. 56.

About the Author/Illustrator

Photo of Author in kayak

Having worked for more than twenty years as a psychologist, teaching courses in Yoga/Meditation, Mediation, and Bereavement, and facilitating personal/spiritual growth workshops and retreats, Fran Laurie Olsen has spent her entire professional career helping people, and teaching them how to find their center and breathe through even the most trying circumstances.

Nature has inspired Olsen, and her creative endeavours, since she was a young girl. Writing short stories and poetry, drawing, painting, and taking photos, she finally has the luxury of pursuing that inspiration full-time, and the perfect location in which to do so. Living right on the river outside of Montreal, in a house overlooking a wetland area with abundant wildlife, Olsen enjoys spending time with her husband (and their cat Theo), kayaking, birding, gardening, and communing with the natural world that surrounds them.

To learn more go to: www.transformationspapillon.com

*Look for the soon to be published book of poems and images: Soul Journeys Series: Exploring the Depths

CPSIA information can be obtained at www.ICGtesting.com
Printed in the USA
BVIW12n1442181115
427520BV00001B/1

9781460267042